PRAISE FOR *BECOMING GHOST*

"Cathy Linh Che's *Becoming Ghost* is a new masterpiece of American love lyric, in the vein of Rita Dove's timeless *Thomas and Beulah* or Ilya Kaminsky's *Deaf Republic*. Love: 'To misunderstand / each other, but to stick around.' Love: 'I mapped our escape.' Love: 'I knew you in your bowl cut, the red car in the driveway, the lens of your father's eye.' I'm getting goosebumps just typing. Che is a mighty poet, nimble across a variety of forms and voices, with a dazzling instinct for how one image, line, photograph, might illuminate the next. *Becoming Ghost* is an indelible reminder of all the people, known and unknown, who loved us enough to survive."

—Kaveh Akbar, author of *Martyr!* and *Pilgrim Bell*

"Cathy Linh Che's *Becoming Ghost* magnifies how the golden shovel form both buries and unearths a poem's roots. Sentences unfold down Che's line breaks, generating shadow scripts and ghost dialogues in a language hidden 'like gold poured / into a molar / or cotton gauze / stuffed into a cheek.' These poems reconcile myth and history, inheritance and upheaval, reconfiguring family memoir as a vehicle for empathy, experimentation, and recovery. *Becoming Ghost* is a marvel of form and spirit."

—Terrance Hayes, author of *So to Speak* and *American Sonnets for My Past and Future Assassin*

"'Dance is a body's refusal / to die,' writes Cathy Linh Che in this gorgeous and searing second collection of poems, the culmination of a long-anticipated multivalence project—one that vivifies her parents' experience being recruited as extras in the Coppola film *Apocalypse Now*. The poems in *Becoming Ghost* stun—they affirm and recenter those exiled from the rusted foundations of American mythology, they refuse to back away as they build new structures to reckon with not just our history but our present. These poems don't just sing: they break my heart and reaffirm life in the same long and glorious breath."

—Sally Wen Mao, author of *Ninetails* and *The Kingdom of Surfaces*

"Cathy Linh Che's poetry vibrates with the rage and ache that accompany revisionist history work. The way she takes Coppola and the exploitative *Apocalypse Now* to task left me agape—these poems break the grammars of male and white-centric narratives."

—Diana Khoi Nguyen, author of *Root Fractures* and *Ghost Of*

T0349418

Also by Cathy Linh Che

Split

An Asian American A to Z: A Children's Guide to Our History

BECOMING GHOST

CATHY LINH CHE

**WASHINGTON
SQUARE PRESS**

ATRIA

New York   Amsterdam/Antwerp   London   Toronto   Sydney/Melbourne   New Delhi

WASHINGTON SQUARE PRESS

ATRIA

An Imprint of Simon & Schuster, LLC
1230 Avenue of the Americas
New York, NY 10020

First Washington Square Press/Atria Paperback edition April 2025

WASHINGTON SQUARE PRESS **/ATRIA** BOOKS and colophon are registered trademarks of Simon & Schuster, LLC

Simon & Schuster strongly believes in freedom of expression and stands against censorship in all its forms. For more information, visit BooksBelong.com.

For information about special discounts for bulk purchases, please contact Simon & Schuster Special Sales at 1-866-506-1949 or business@simonandschuster.com.

The Simon & Schuster Speakers Bureau can bring authors to your live event. For more information or to book an event, contact the Simon & Schuster Speakers Bureau at 1-866-248-3049 or visit our website at www.simonspeakers.com.

Interior design by Davina Mock-Maniscalco

Manufactured in the United States of America

1 3 5 7 9 10 8 6 4 2

Library of Congress Control Number: 2024052158

ISBN 978-1-6680-8892-0
ISBN 978-1-6680-8893-7 (ebook)

For my family

Contents

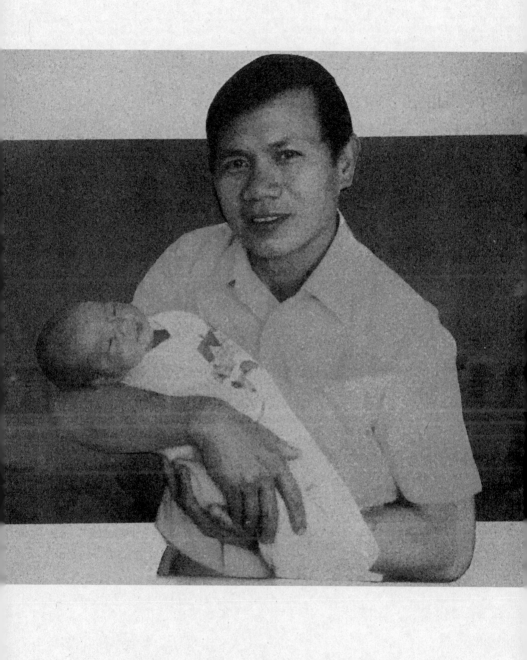

Becoming Ghost

I stand behind a one-way mirror.
My father sits in a room
interrogating himself.

Bright bulb shining
like the idea
of a daughter.

————————

It looked just like the real
thing. The helicopters,
the fields, the smoke

which rose in colors,
the bullets blank,
but too real.

Coppola yelled, *Action!*,
and we dragged slowly
across the back of the screen,

miniature prisoners of war
to Robert Duvall's
broad naked chest.

What you'll never see
written into the credits
are our names.

_____

Ghost of a daughter,
specter, spectator,
from a future

we could only dream of.
I'd never dreamt
that one day

you'd be my age
and too bitter
to talk to me.

I who gave every peso
to your mother,
who sewed coins

into the linings
of my pockets
so that you could eat

enough food
and grow taller
than either one of us.

I am asking you
to look me in the face
and say, *Father*.

I am
asking you
to see me.

———————

Morning yawns and today
my father has deleted a daughter.
Today he's blessed with two sons.

Today he may be haunted
by the grip of a friend
who died in his arms

but not the scent of a baby girl
he held years ago. *Women*,
he says, and spits.

There is plasm, he says,
and shrugs—*and then*
there is ectoplasm. What is a father

who has two sons? *Happy*,
he says with a toothpick pressed
between his thumb

and forefinger. *Happy*, he says,
looking into the mirror
and seeing no reflection.

Becoming Ghost

In Sài Gòn, I wore
my áo dài sidesaddle

on my husband's xe Honda,
the atmosphere a slurry

of exhaust
and humidity.

My hair dragged
like a black curtain

through traffic.
Engines riled,

multiplying.
Already, it's early.

Here, Coppola
dresses down,

shirtless, less
fancy director,

more man of the people
gone jungle wild.

Gray waves zipper
along the shore.

Coppola says, *I want it to smell*
like the real thing.

I want to tell him,
The real thing

is a landscape
of work and death,

the names of our ancestors
slack in our mouths,

just the art of loving
your family line enough

to reproduce it.

Zombie Apocalypse Now: The Walking Dead

Dawn crows, and I shave
the ache from my face.

_____

The wind, a susurration of flocks.

My love keens,
it calls. Guttural, it weeps.
An elegy. Another elegy.

We arrow our way
through the present. Sometimes
it's all we have.

The morning rising
boldly again. I open my mouth
to forget getting soaked.

I let it hammer down.

_____

The tectonic universe shifts,

and we are forced to move
like birds fleeing the seasons.

I will not move,
not today.

Scrum of the afternoon,
loud bark in the distance.

If I must tessellate this aloneness,
it is this I most crave,

to be done
with aubades.

I want to stay here,
with you,

our backs against the water,
starlings blotting out the sky.

———————————

I press my palms to my eyes
and imagine a bloodless world.

What moves through me
is just wind and your breath.

I hold it as we march toward
our own lives,

toward a stillness
quilted with leaves.

––––––––––––

I was used to surviving
on scraps.

I was afraid
of losing sentience,

losing myself
to an other.

You became
another life

I could lose.

––––––––––––

They asked me to follow
the script.

My death written
before I was born.

When the director yelled *Cut!*
a whole life evacuated me.

I stepped out of the skin
of a man I played for seven years,

into the sunshine of a life
called Steven Yeun.

Left my pregnant TV wife behind.
Left the heat of the South behind.

Like a door I shut,
I leave that world behind.

My downfall
for someone else's rise.

Classic love story.
Sacrifice.

I rip the spine in half
and burn the last page.

————————

Mid-shoot, we found out
our papers were ready.

We bused west
back to Manila.

Three years later,
in Los Angeles,

our sponsor brought us
to the ArcLight

so that we could
watch ourselves

edited out
of the frame.

The film won
Academy Awards.

We were never saved.
I've been directing

my home video opus.
They'll never detect my rage.

———————————

Child,
I couldn't
imagine you—

born into a world haunted
not by ghosts
but carcasses that stunk

through the pall
of each dream.
I stared into the cracked

riverbed, the driest dirt.
Your life was nothing
I could fathom

from the hell
we kept
escaping.

———————————

What is the opposite of elegy
but birth announcement?

Santa Monica winks at me—
all the stars, all that light.

Today I will be a father.

I hear in the moon's pulse,
an ocean.

I watch in the sunrise,
a new sun.

Bomb that tree line back about a hundred yards. Give me room to breathe.

a golden shovel

Daughter, I think you embellish what you don't know. A bomb
is nothing like a slammed door. That
is just your poetic imagination. Have you seen a tree
disappear into flames? That's what a bomb can do. I taught you, line
by line, my own poetry. It was a song back
when I went hungry. Your grandmother died when I was about
to turn ten. I became an orphan then. I made sure that you never went without a
meal. I taught you to count to one hundred
in Vietnamese. You played in backyards,
on swing sets, bright shards of grass at your feet. I tried to give
you the safety I never had. And now, you tell me
that you are afraid of me? You lock yourself in your room
and write my story. I'm here, waiting to
be acknowledged. Can you hear me breathe?

Becoming Ghost

Sundays, my parents drink a single can of beer.
Is this love, I think. To share what is bitter

one evening of the week. To misunderstand
each other, but to stick around?

I've wept over someone as gone as the stars
which flecked the sky in Joshua Tree years ago.

He said I'd stripped him bare. Sometimes,
my cousin placed his finger there. Some days,

memory won't go. Some days, I feel whole.
When the stars burned off, we were left with desert heat.

He slept alone in the tent as I hid in the car to write.
He looked uncomfortable, knees bent up in sleep.

Mornings, I gazed at his face to lock it there.
Reproductions I'd flyered across each calendar square.

I felt him awake on the earth's other side.
The moon glowed huge above the horizon.

In Seoul, the humidity, thick as rags.
My nails freshly painted some god-awful hue.

I unattached a single drop of sweat from his neck.
The blazing orange of the sky in Malaysia

he couldn't bring himself to watch. Just ordered
another beer to share. Things have a way of cycling.

Perhaps it was Sunday and I thought we could
become my parents. I nursed his indifferent body.

He no longer held me in sleep. I want to collapse
what we were, fold it all the way in.

It is difficult to end a poem
with the word pain.

Cargo

I don't want to carry the weight
of my father's war, the machinery,
monsoon rains, oxen turned over

and blood in the paddy. He cracked
our bowls and dented the linoleum.
Our door nearly leapt off the hinge.

I watched my father switch my brother
to bits. Father, god of the forge, spun
the metal, quick and hot. We melted

toy soldiers to watch the flames
burst up. Stoop-shouldered and tense,
he built an uneasy mythology.

Soldier who ate grasshoppers and ants,
fished with men who sucked on cigarettes—
of engines and planes and hang gliders

which fell in flight from the bluffs of La Jolla
and into the epic wind. War is the season
that moved him around. From orphan

to the sea, from Qui Nhon
to the Philippines. War is a word
I can't stuff twenty years into.

What utterances can I translate,
what story, whose teeth buried,
and what brittle child's bones?

There's a silhouette where
my family will fit. The story I trim
with scissors. My father I cut to scraps.

Go

Because the birds sculpted
the air with their song,

I sent that flash across the sea.
Candle in a paper lantern,

the flame rose and dipped.

———————

I've been hiding
from my father.

Fog-damp pall over the city.
I ink this bruise onto paper.

Years ago, in Highland Park,
we picnicked in the backyard.

We slept in the living room.
I clung to my beautiful mother.

Flipped the pillow and pressed
against its coolness.

I held grudges like tiny fists
full of sand, then, let go.

I kissed the sky and the air
and ocean's cobalt hue.

―――――――

Murky alphabet,

I falter the letter,
I elide the gaps.

If the opalescent dew
meant anything,

it meant that one day,
I'd be lifted above my feelings.

You'd become less than
a feeling, the way every lover

I've known no longer hurts me.
Those old charges detonated.

―――――――

Here and now, I make room for joy.
Birds ribbon the air with their singing.

Their voices riot up. The planes
with their hulking engines—

they fly too. Your lips—I uninterrupt.
I charley horse and miracle ride

your absence. Puddle of salt water,
shivering wound. Seaweed, we sing

of losses. Cold under this blanket,
I am waiting for an alarm to sing.

———————

I've polished this anger and now it's a knife.
I'm hardened as a hunter
ornamenting his cave

with the bones of the dead.
I'm so sick of history
dragging behind me.

I don't want to be sad.
But my father has retreated
and the lashes across his back

have not healed and
he could have killed himself
and we'd be blamed.

We stood barefoot on the street,
listening to my father smash
against the garage walls.

I fling stones
into the ether.
I wash my hands in ink.

The lost-in-the-fog body
born of matter,
history-less,

untethered.
Better to be alive
and bewildered.

At least I can name the thing.
To love my father
is to love his wounds.

In times like these,
we present our hurts
like old toys we polish up

to show each other
who we used to be.

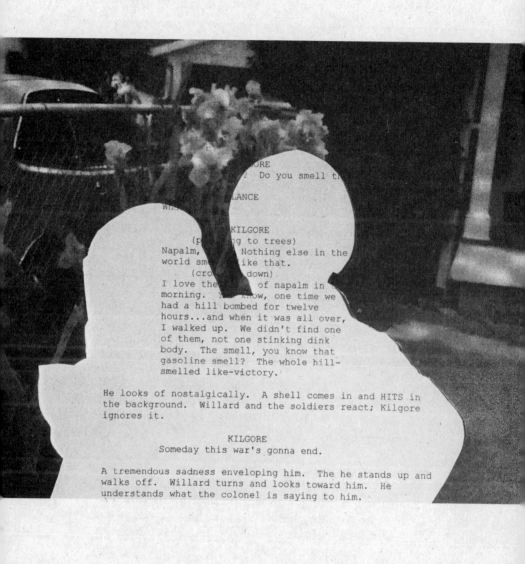

                              ORE
                         ? Do you smell t

                    ANCE
        W

                         KILGORE
                (p   g to trees)
        Napalm,   Nothing else in the
        world sm   ike that.
                (cro   down)
        I love the   of napalm in
        morning.   ow, one time we
        had a hill bombed for twelve
        hours...and when it was all over,
        I walked up. We didn't find one
        of them, not one stinking dink
        body. The smell, you know that
        gasoline smell? The whole hill-
        smelled like-victory.

He looks of nostalgically. A shell comes in and HITS in
the background. Willard and the soldiers react; Kilgore
ignores it.

                         KILGORE
        Someday this war's gonna end.

A tremendous sadness enveloping him. The he stands up and
walks off. Willard turns and looks toward him. He
understands what the colonel is saying to him.

Zombie Apocalypse Now: Survival

The air was blurry-wet
when the undead arrived,

a director with his crew,
the camera with its red eye

trained on us,
ready to devour

our Vietnam War–fresh brains
for their American art.

We didn't have lines,
we were "extras."

We'd survived a war
to be cast into the margins

of our own story.
They say that cameras

steal your souls.
Sometimes, they do.

Sometimes, they pay
minimum wage,

which is more
per hour

than I earned
an entire year

working as an apprentice
to a tailor.

Perhaps, three months pregnant
and not showing,

I threw myself
onto the dirt

again and again,
pretending

to be shot
in the back.

To the viewer,
I was dead.

I felt dead.
My lover

left me behind
for Paris

with his real wife
and his newborn son

christened Philip
for the Philippines,

where he was born,
on a bus on the way

to Mandaluyong
in a refugee camp

just north
of Manila.

The palms
grow verdant,

in thick clumps
over the gun-gray river.

In this fertile air,
everything shoots up.

The movie men
planted rigging

into the ground,
so much napalm

faked: It looked
just like

the real thing.

FADE IN: EXT.

a golden shovel

I chew my dinner carefully. A
helicopter arrives. The single
man at the table is my father. The image
of his younger self fades, then a faint scent of
Baler. So I walk in the forest listening to trees.

———————

My aunt asked her son to serve us coconut
cut from a cluster of trees
out front. For the time being
it is 2011. History is being viewed
on the television, through
the eyes of a white American. The
fact is, my parents were barely visible through the veil
of that gaze. They were the props of
empire. Characters with short time
and no lines. Or
props to smell like a
real thing. Movie so real, it's beyond a dream.

———————

While directing, Coppola occasionally
chomped on a lime-colored

mango, skin and all. Film was all smoke

and rigging, wafts

of bright sulfur through

salt spray and surf-ready waves. The

scene opens just outside the frame.

My mother sleeping in a room, scented with yellow

droplets of piss. How then

she lay, bathed in violet.

———————

The music

blares. A speaker begins

to call like a child, quietly

at first, then pitching toward howl. Silence, suggestive

of taxidermy. Mother of

God, pray for my mother in 1968,

13 and sent away—

waiting for the year to become, finally, 1969.

Then, perhaps

she listens to the

radio, through to the end

of the evening. By

the time she wakes, my father is already gone. The

scene opens just outside the doors

———————

of the schoolhouse. I can see him now,

walking toward the beach, moving

past fishermen selling their catch, through

the crew members setting up cameras to capture the

morning's just-rinsed light. He waits to enter the frame.

The director asks, Are

you ready? My father climbs aboard a helicopter, which skids

across the shore. He considers his role of

an interpreter. His English, his training as a mechanic. The helicopters,

borrowed from Marcos (Ferdinand, not

Imelda), swerve. The Hueys that

Coppola used to stage the war suddenly needed to put down rebels. We

wait, my father says. But we receive payment. Still, we do what we can—

keep busy, practice English, prepare to make

a life somewhere new. My mother insists that filming was fun for them,

a way out

of the boredom of the camp. As

I listen to their telling, I realize that

my version doesn't match theirs, though

I take what I can. Along the way, I discover a lost uncle. Rather

than seeking hard

fact (after all, he may still be alive somewhere), I record the shapes

of my family's feeling: the guilt that

stays, the glide

when I press my mother, who by

now engages with the narrative at

a distance, with the triggered up-close at random

intervals. She pastes album after album of photographs, then

marked *Cathy Linh Che, 1980–*, a

nod to a gravestone, in defiance of (or an elegy for?) a phantom

country. The construct as real as a helicopter

exploding ceremoniously when her friend from camp tosses her straw hat in.

Her face in full,

handsomely paid view.

In Baler, a surfboard floats

atop a few waves, right by

"Charlie's Point." The

guide drives me via sidecar to a grove of palm trees

when the scene from the film comes at me suddenly.

"Napalm" dropped along this ridge. River mouth without

vine or cover. The charred remains warning

my mother about the

life ahead of her: a jungle

in flames. Mortar fire bursts,

only, it's just a dream she carries into

America, and only when I ask her a

question. Her answers are never reluctant, bright

with detail, as if illuminated by red-orange

fire, her past scorched in a glob

of sticky heat. In exchange, 80 pesos for a day of

acting work. Just playing life anew, napalm

that never burned her, even though she lived inside that flame.

I chew my dinner carefully. The

year is 1976. My parents sleep on a cot. The view

outside: beach waves curling. After three moves,

my parents ready themselves for a bus ride across

Luzon, back to Manila, in preparation for the

journey at last to Los Angeles. My grandmother burning

incense, praying for her daughter. She combs the trees

for meaning as

she lies in her hospital bed, wrapped in the

loss of a gone daughter who won't return until 1993. Smoke

forgives the distance. That ghostly

veil. In Los Angeles, the helicopters

spotlight another car on the run. It will crash come

morning in the most congested city in the world. I stop the tape and

empty a vase of its water. From here, where to go?

In the kitchen, recounting

My daughter calls me,
hungry for a story.

I feed her fish and soup
and greens cut from the garden.

She asks for my story [private].
She asks for my story [public].

I ask her to translate what it is she needs.

———

The city was not the country.
In the country, bombs fell at night.

In the morning, water buffalo
lay on their sides, dead.

———

I love the smell of napalm . . .

a golden shovel

Did I see napalm explode? All the time! Napalm

flames, their greasy fingers in the air. I wasn't a son

drafted into the war, just a daughter to marry off. After Americans arrived, nothing

was left of my grandfather's home. What else

do you expect when tanks roll in?

Translate the

word. Na Pom. Oh. Yes, the bombed world.

Today, I enter my garden, teeming with smells,

basil and lemongrass. Dragon fruit climbing over the trellis, reptile-like,

waxy and succulent. Guava that

swells under my watch. Once, a South Vietnamese soldier—I

knew him from the village—stumbled into our home. War takes everything we love.

He was shot by the Việt Cộng. I watched the

man bleed out into the sheets. It was the fresh smell

of death that got me. Flash forward: Scene of

myself on a film set. I was the Việt Cộng. I was the scenery. "Napalm"

explodes up. I heard bom, bom, bom shaking in

my fists. Couldn't sleep last night. Who could sleep through a strafing, the

sounds echoing bom, bom, bom, from that day, into this morning.

Becoming Ghost

I unhook the photograph
from its nail,
needle the aperture,

and find my youth
history, a washout
of dieting and wedding cake.

In those days,
I dreamt less
of a private bedchamber

and more a future
without smoke.
I sleep on this slab of a bed

in the town of Baler,
in an elementary
schoolhouse rented out.

Coppola asks
that I execute
a facsimile

of an adjacent life.
What a relief
to play the enemy

and to find her
a frightened 22-year-old
shooting a machine gun

at a UH-1 Huey.
Revenge foretells my living
well. In those days,

I was frugal with words,
opting to hide them
like gold poured

into a molar
or cotton gauze
stuffed into a cheek

to stave off the rattle
bitten into
my gums.

December 3, 1975

a golden shovel

My mother wakes early
to go to church. Dawn
redux. Her áo dài is Virgin Mary blue.
Her hair is still long, reflecting light.
A border control officer filters
through her documents, preparing to send her through
to their new home destination. The
casting call goes out in the meantime: Paid extras needed for jungle
defoliation scene. *Apocalypse Now* and
Hearts of Darkness play across
the screen of my mother's face. I glimpse a flicker, a
flare, then the sudden foul
odor of napalm and oil in the swamp.

————————

In the opening scene, a
man showers. The mist
rises and clings
to the blue tarp, temporary walls to
maintain the privacy of the
100 refugees at the Jose Fabella Center. Trees
flank the main road. This
stay could
last forever, or it could be

a stopgap before the

repatriation of our protagonist—back to the jungle

where he would have spent a decade of

his 30s into 40s being tortured in a

reeducation camp, lucky to not be one of 3.9 million

dead. He scrubs off his 12 years

as a soldier, a long 6 months ago.

_____

Dissolve. Our

protagonists in a small boat. View

of my mother's pallid face. The camera moves

to the sea, as the boat drifts closer

toward land in the distance. Through

starlight, then dawnlight, the

journey begins its eighth day. Mist

burns off. Cut to my mother tilting

a canteen toward her lips. She drinks down

seasickness. Cut to

Sê, visibly pregnant, clinging to the

edge as the boat lurches over a wave. Cut to my father cooking cháo cá over a tepid

fire, then, my mother unloading a mouthful of bile into the water.

Becoming Ghost

I lived
in the cement house
I fed the chickens
from my plate
their claws
scratched
new marks
I carried my son
in a bucket
my daughter
in another
balanced them
on a pole
mortar fire overhead
the German nuns
took my newborn
I had no colostrum
no pearl of milk
he calls out
for something
I could not give
I threshed
the thin grains
of rice from their
brown husks

Q & A

My grandmother.

Who was she?

A stranger.

Why strange?

War, I guess, and time.

What will razing history do?

I want to bridge the distance.

She may have given you
salt plums?

Watermelon, mustard greens, fish-salt
drying on the salt plum air.

Irretrievable, this
grandmother.

She is a ghost.

Wisped inside of you,
egg drop soup.

Eaten up.

You are ravenous.

Not satisfied.

Not sated.

I haven't disappeared.

You're here.

Were flowers on her casket?

Did you wear white?

My mother did. She was a good/bad
daughter.

Like Antigone.

No, not like Antigone. She received the
telegram from Vietnam, but did not
return home to bury her dead.

In a dust storm, she was—
like Antigone.

Dear America

In '76, my parents' bewildered arrival.
The grocery stores, all that refrigerated meat.
The houses without basements or shelters

where my mother slept, or did not sleep, while
American bombs called overhead. The dirt flying
up. What hope did my mother have then

but the life she carried. Her body.
The decay in the ocean. America, look
at my mother's face, and love her.

My father, too, with his dark hands.
He lived in Virginia, aviator glasses,
a Marlon Brando. America, his dream.

Who made him love white faces,
wish his children's futures
as flags of surrender?

Little sailboats released into a harbor
toward a horizon of false equality.
America, you ask for our light.

We give it to ourselves, our loves,
our kerosene hearts lamp-lit
for the children to come.

I love the smell of napalm . . .

a golden shovel

From the hospital bed, I watch Bê nap. Alm-
ighty God, why did I give my newborn son
to that German convent? Nothing
prepared me for the wreck. Who else
could take him in? He wailed in
the hallway. Bê sang to him but couldn't calm the
colic. Hoa across the world
now, or perhaps dead at sea. The room smells
of powdered milk. It was like
a punishment, how my breasts produced not a drop. I was furious that
nobody would take the baby in. I
was diagnosed tim yêú. My body betrayed the love
I had for the boy. Some nights in the
chirring of crickets, in the smell
of the damp paddy, I hear the voice of
my son speak to me in German. A palm
reader predicted that I would suffer. In
war, we all suffer. The
inevitability of this mourning.

The Extras' Commentary

We were transported
on a C-47 cargo plane
from the refugee camp

in Mandaluyong
to the filming site
at Baler River.

Even if we didn't film
on a particular day,
we were paid.

The refugee camp
was set up
in an abandoned

mental hospital.
It was beautifully
made.

The Extras' Commentary

I immigrated to the US
on June 18, 1976.

We filmed
from May to June.

We were paid 12
or 13 dollars a day.

When I came
to the United States,

I made $2.10 an hour,
minimum wage.

The Extras' Commentary

I bought a tael of gold
with my extra money. Also,
a radio, a watch, some clothes.
Before the film, I had two shirts,
two pairs of pants: one for wearing,
one for the wash.
During our first escape attempt,
I left my suitcase on the boat.
The owner called the Việt Cộng.
I went to jail. I lost my clothes.
I went to Sài Gòn. I wore my gold wedding ring.
I asked your aunt to help me sell it
for fabric, which I sewed into another set.

Los Angeles, Manila, Đà Nẵng

California drought withering the basins,
the hills ready to ignite. Oh, silly ways

I've loved and unraveled myself.
I, a parched field, and not a spit of rain.

I announced to a room of strangers,
I've never loved anyone more.

Now he and I no longer speak.
Outside: Manila, 40 years

after my parents' first arrival.
I deplane where they debarked.

In 1975, my parents received
fishermen's lunches, a bottle

of fish sauce. They couldn't enter
until they were vaccinated.

My mother, 21, newly emptied
of a stillborn daughter.

In Đà Nẵng, my cousin
has become unrecognizable

after my four-year absence.
His teeth, at 21, have begun to rot.

His face swollen over.
I want to shield him

from his difficult life.
Tased at 15 by the cops

until he pissed himself.
So beaten in the mental institution

that family had to
bring him home.

His mother always near tears
when I ask, How are you doing?

You want to know what
survivorhood looks like?

It's not romantic.
The corn drying huskless

in the front yard.
The ducks chasing

each other in the back.
The thick arms

of a woman who will carry bricks
for the rest of her life.

The bricks aren't a metaphor
for the weight she carries.

Ánh, which means light,
is sick, and cannot work,

but instead goes wandering the neighborhood,
eating other people's food, bloating

his mother's unpayable debts.
My mother stopped crying years ago.

What's the use, she says, of all this leaking.
Enough to fill a drainage ditch, a reservoir?

No, just enough to wet a pillow.
My uncles and their browned skins,

not a pinch of fat anywhere.
They work the fields and swallow

beer after beer, getting sentimental.
Whose birds have come to roost,

whose pigs in the muck?
Their dog has just birthed four new pups.

Despite ourselves, time walks on.
I strolled lovers' lane with my cousin.

The heart-lights reflected on the river's black.
The locks clustered and dangling.

I should have left our names on that bridge.
My name, the names of my family, written there.

City of the Future

Nopales   the sun
bleached each paddle   we scavenged
     iron filings from the dirt—

after the spring rains
   indigo rising   what searchbeams
shined over the water's cobalt

     in the city of the future, whose land
and whose landlocked prism?   in the refugee camp
     clobbered by monsoon rains

   then boredom   we ectomorphed
we countryless   the rice rotten
the unfresh meat   I gathered opo seeds

   and dried them   in my pockets
planted them uprooted   a new garden
   to feed the hungry dirt

Ode to

I broke a dish
against the floor and called it
family. I shut the window
to seal in my loneliness.
Beyond the blue wilderness,
beyond the moonlight,
there was me in a Los Angeles
kitchen, being fed by Lorenzo,
who nearly died of pneumonia
days before. I watched as
he slept on his bed, his head
atop the pillow,
the red flush, I hoped,
of health. I'm telling you
that the beams of his arms
anchored us, as he whistled
(what is that sound?)
through his teeth, told me,
Cathy es la bonita.
I want to tell you a story
of my body. I did not believe
myself to be beautiful.
I stood and smiled
at the camera. I watched
the sun stare back.
Only the tortilla's steam.

The carne and the gristle,

tang of onion releasing into my throat.

Though money claps

its applause, though the world

praises its dirty green scent,

I think of love, of home,

the not-yet-gone afternoon,

when I returned

to eat, to drink—to a time

when home was here, and leaving

seemed unfathomable.

Meals

I hear the wet click of bones unfastening,
my mother's hands slick with fat.

Green the leaves that stuck to my hands
when I washed them in the silver bowl.

Translucent the cartilage between my teeth.
The whole burnt summer, I tasted the cactus,

I tasted the dirt. Tortillas warmed over the stove,
arrows pointed from the burner, a slice of American

cheese melted in between. Like any good prayer,
my mother taught me to eat well.

Martha chopped the onions, spraying acid. I teared up
when I crossed her kitchen, tiles cold against my feet.

In their backyard, José washed tomatillos
of their paper skins. I held the hand my father

used to squeeze blood from my mother's—
I tasted a knife I licked clean.

Aunt Bê leaves fruit bedside.
I stain my thumbnail with sap.

I smell Đà Nẵng's salt air. The ocean
like a bath, everyone out before 7 a.m.,

before the sun can crisp our skin like roast duck.
Before I am coffee with condensed milk.

After the wedding, red pumpkin seeds
like spent firecrackers across the floor.

This is when I begin. When history teaches
an apprentice he is less than a bowl of rice.

When hunger blunts his growth
and gnaws down the fat,

so that he is all sinew and muscle
raising three fleshy Americans.

When ice is a luxury
to water down beer.

I begin with quail feed and pig feed.
With fish netted from the sea.

With scales shimmering against the walls of the sink.
I gnaw on the bones like a good dog.

Once I dreamt I was swallowed by a snake.
The snake was an immigrant household.

We filled our stomachs until they belled.
We ate until we pealed.

We unsecreted our history.
We wrote out our meager mouths.

Poem Before a Verdict

Once, in Long Beach,
when my mother said,
No English,

the solicitor told her
to go back to the jungle
where she came from.

She taught me
the names of flowers.
Years later

I learned
their names
in English—

narcissus,
rhododendron,
chrysanthemum.

The words placed me
firmly
in this country,

though I slipped
from one language
to the other, amphibian.

Once, as a child,
I coughed and ear-ached
and cried in a new home.

Tora! Tora! Tora! thundered
on the television. Warplanes
dropped bombs like so much

weight. My parents slept
in that blue light. Their
eyelids shuddered.

I imagined
that light to be
another country.

What do the men see
when they say *Ni hao*
and *Konnichiwa*?

A police officer
once aimed his eye up
the length of my leg

as I descended
the subway stairs.
What could I do then?

When I was a girl,
my mother was arrested
and placed in a cell.

The officer did not cuff her
in front of us
because we surrounded her

like small animals
reciting the tricks
we learned at school.

Hoa Thi Leche,
she wrote in her ledger.
Leche means milk,

I said proudly.
The officer
smiled down

at me. Soldiers called
my grandmother
mama-san.

She was a lucky one,
just one lost son,
one lost daughter,

and grandchildren
who grew limbs
in another country,

where they spoke
the language of soldiers.
Their eyes shone

with the milk
their motherland
could not afford.

Today, I am singing
their songs: chorus
of my mother's heartbreaks,

my father a soldier
in a long-ago war,
my brother's voice

ricocheting
through the phone line
on October 10,

when he was held at gunpoint
in Liberty Park.
Don't tell mom,

he says. He wears
a bracelet, etched
10/10 to remember.

Soldiers touched my mother's hair.
My great-grandfather was cut down
by an American plane.

My mother says, *In Vietnam,*
a life means so little.
What does a life mean in America?

Live-Stream

Keep watch. Turn the camera.
Dilate. In our hundreds,
our thousands. Our millions.

Eaten. Have you? Slept?
To the activists who fought
for me. Did my family

die less? Are families dying
less today, as I send poetry money
to buy food and tents?

Last year, the average
American paid $5,109
to the U.S. military.

Death could not be funded
without us. In our thousands.
Our millions. Our munitions.

I go to the literary
nonprofit party.
I smile into the camera.

Step and repeat.
I touch phones,
exchange contacts.

What does our refusal
look like? Over plates
of donated cheese and wine.

Over the meat of a killed lamb.
If I can eat, I must ask. Have you?
Eaten yet? Slept?

I, in my warm
rent-stabilized apartment,
my radiator heat.

You, wet through the winter.
Turn the camera,
back and forth.

——

From the karaoke room,
I sing,
I will survive.

I was barred
from learning
music

by my mother,
who tabulated
the cost

of violin rentals
and after-school lessons
against the labor

of each dress
she assembled.
I have chased music

my whole life. Learned
from my nerdy friends
in a public library

how to bounce
my shoulders,
roll my hips.

Now, I'm in love
with a composer.
He sees a guitar

and hears sound.
I see language
as syllabics

and breath,
two bodies moving
balletically past

one another
inside my bathroom's
narrow strictures.

At protests,
he'd beat the drums
as the students marched

demanding answers
for what happened
to the disappeared.

Music,
the heartbeat
of a movement.

——

Our dead on screen,
a freeze, a scroll.
Journalists hungry,

but reporting.
I weigh my eating
at a restaurant

against helping
someone else eat.
Sometimes,

I stay home. Sometimes,
I watch my credit
balloon, collect

reading fees and jurying,
banking this against
a zero interest card

that will charge 22%
come June. I have read
the budget proposal,

the cost of bombing
five countries,
disinvestment,

collapsing tourism,
start-up capital withering,
credit downgrade.

I join your risk
so that you
are less alone.

Turn
the camera,
back and forth.

I write to you
from the afterlife
of near-annihilation.

Zombie Apocalypse Now: Pandemic

During the novel virus spread that
could kill my mother, she cackles,
impish. She has enough

toilet paper in the shed out back
to last six months. From every trip
to Costco, every coupon for Charmin,

every sale at ABC Supermarket
and 99 Ranch—my mother has
enough food, water, and paper

to last the apocalypse.
Even if the paper were to run out,
she still remembers how to do it,

with leaves or dried clumps of dirt
scavenged along the way
to the outhouse.

In Vietnamese,
to take a shit is đi cầu—
to go to the bridge.

To drop your meal into
the mouths of fish congregating
in the churning river below.

In LA, the stores have rationed
one of each item per person.
My mother has lived through

enough curfews and lockdowns
to know to be ready for the moment.
Limits are meant to be gamed.

She's lived a life of scrimping,
saving. She lives for
the exquisite pleasure

of squeezing more
from the oozing meat
of a copper penny.

July is watermelon season.

Promise we will rebuild
painted on the concrete.

Promise we will return.
Sure as the cactus, hardy,

survives the desert,
the prickly orange-gold

sunsets shall glow.
Even without water,

the plants will grow.
The olive trees

will return. Wild thyme
will sprout through

the stone slabs.
Roses spraying across

the remnants of a house.
Planting for me is a form

of resistance. I bring life
to the earth, Medo said,

as he pressed the black,
tear-shaped seeds into the sand.

When you live an earnest,
beloved life, you never die.

Watermelon vines take root.
Fruit sweetening in the sun.

Empires will fall.
Palestine will be free.

Only fools are hopeful. I am
that fool.

Zombie Apocalypse Now: On Love

The year of the Geneva Accords,
       I was conceived, dead
in the center of a splitting country.

Water dragged my legs back to shore.
       Out to sea, I never learned to swim.
My husband cast me in his escape fantasy.

I bore his children from a split.
       He captured them all on Super 8.
Photography is, after all, painting with light.

I never wanted to be a movie star,
       just a wife.
My mother was a widow for 13 years.

When she remarried,
       I couldn't see beyond
losing her to another love.

I mist the plants in the garden.
       Water beads
on the waxy skin of each tomato.

Plants don't run off
      the way daughters do.
They stay, greening. They fruit.

I answered the call—
      beautiful, dutiful wife.
I didn't read the script.

Zombie Apocalypse Now: Prelude

On the boat, we fled the hordes.

In the rearview, zombies ate up
the left-behind as they escaped.

The Americans evacuated
three years prior.

Tanks rolled into the capital.
A new flag was raised.

For 11 months,
we were without a country.

We were cast into a film
about our own apocalypse.

We were diligent in our portrayal.

Zombie Apocalypse Now: In the Viewing Hall

In the viewing hall,
    the videos streamed.

Zombies on one side,
    survivors on the other.

Bloody steaks served up
    by NGO do-gooders,

trying to broker a peace
    decades after.

Blue-gray rain plucked at the roof.
    The lights dimmed.

Vibrating on-screen, an amateur
    documentary about friendship.

The forks clinked as everyone chewed.
    In the survivors' chests

scenes played and replayed
    their lovers devoured.

Seasons of this.
   Their bruised faces,

their moans, not language,
   but lowing id.

Zombie Apocalypse Now: Revival

I wait to be reanimated.
        Love is like that—

resurrecting you from the dead.
        I step off the conveyor belt

in the people factory.
        Each fleshy mannequin

with its polished sex,
        promising domesticity.

I begin to feel monstrous,
        arranging and rearranging

the pantry. Inside my mouth
        is an unfillable hole.

I have tried to be a friend to myself.
        I have used both hands.

My mother cooks my father meals
        and stitches his shirts.

They watch K-dramas
        together on the couch.

My mother calls me with new gossip.
     I listen to her refrain.

I unzip, waiting to be eaten.
     I look into the mirror,

and it looks back at me
     the same.

Zombie Apocalypse Now: Documentary

My father and I
are terrible

codirectors—he and I both
yank the narrative

toward our own
insistent eye.

He held his arms out
like Christ, then whipped

a plumbing snake
across his back.

I refused
to come home.

When is my father no longer
my father?

When Christ descends
and gobbles up his flesh.

My father was a refugee,
fleeing the zombies

that war made
of his own people.

I grab the camera
and make a documentary

about his life. I select
an *Apocalypse Now* film clip,

label it fair use,
pay a voice actor

to play my father
speaking so much English.

Sometimes artifice is necessary
to get closer to the real thing.

The bridge collapses
and the voice actor giggles

reading my father's lines.

I love the smell of napalm . . .

a golden shovel

Dow produced napalm
in the early days of the war. I was without a son—
was losing my daughter. I cradled her for three hours, then her nothing
heartbeat was a flicker I couldn't keep alive, here or else-
where, in my too-large hands. In
the birthing room, I monitored the
EKG until it flatlined. My wife in another world
here in Sài Gòn. Her body still smells
of unwashed scalp. Nurses told me to lie. I held the secret like
a spent match. When my wife woke from the coma, it was her smile that
gutted me. She insisted on buying baby clothes from each passing vendor. I
couldn't watch her spend her love
on a child the
hospital had already buried. I remember my daughter's smell,
viscous with blood, her head of
thick, mucus-bright hair. Around her seemed a corona. Palm
fronds shook outside the window. Monsoon pouring in.
I hoped her body would stay buried under the
mud. I mapped our escape. We'd leave when the rain halted in the morning.

Zombie Apocalypse Now: Talking Dead

I walked through the trees, mourning.

I looked brightness in the eye.
Held a penny on my tongue.

The shock of metal and rust,
its brown-gold sweet.

I roamed the field
angry and burned

asking bitter questions
of a gun.

Dance is a body's refusal
to die. But, oh, your gone hair.

The flame and orange flare.
Barrel, sugar, and stench.

Our forms, our least known
selves,

the stutter of a body's
broken grammar.

Forgiveness

Into the distance recedes my father.
Time recursive as night waves.

A seam riven. The moon filling
like a bladder. Faint areola of light.

I open each window
and in floods the salt air.

Time corrodes the memory box.
The photographs are proof

we once loved
one another.

Is there a place where
forgiveness can return us?

My father tilting a warm bottle,
my head resting against his arm.

The milk-white moon
fills like a bladder.

A seam riven, faint
areola of light.

Time recursive as night waves.
In the distance my father.

——

A stunt double steps in,
      removes his sweater

then his undershirt,
      wraps the plumbing snake

around his hand,
      cracks the greased whip

over his back—*Cut!*

My father, a director now,
      steps in to show him how it's done—

a pink stripe, a red lash—
      Make them say *please.*

Show yourself!
      slick and white underneath

——

I opened the camcorder,
and the cartridge
was gone.

Instead, I digitized
two reels of film,
a VHS cassette, a stack of DVDs,

home videos that flickered
the green of a backyard,
the sway of a swing set,

my brother and I chasing
each other in a circle
on motorized bikes.

Once, my father lectured us
and asked plaintively,
Can we move past this?

Not without an apology, I said.
He prostrated himself, humiliated,
a father having to win back

the regard of his children.
Every lash across
my brother's ass,

every drop squeezed
from the stubborn fruit
of my mother's surprised

finger, every slammed door,
every bowl thrown, every
shout, I've finally let go.

It's a condition of forgetting,
stitching of one kind
of life to another.

——

Screenplay 1: My father becomes
a famous home movie director.
He writes his autobiography.

Screenplay 2: I return to my father's house
and pillage his videos for my use.
They and I will never be forgotten.

Screenplay 3: Coppola scraps
his need to retell *Heart of Darkness*
and gives his millions to the refugees.

Here, he says. *You tell your own story.*

My father filming my brother,
nude, brown, his belly
rounded with milk,

my father pointing to show off
his son. One Christmas
my cousin gifted my father a bundle

of photographs. In one, he sits among
great boulders on a shore in Virginia.
He was well-muscled and shirtless,

a flyboy in aviators,
grinning above the waves.
Absent the smell

of the coiled film
in the canister, absent
the thick white paint

on the bedroom wall where
my father projected film,
I become the lens.

The machine lighting
the dust motes.
I feel the heat of the bulb.

I watch our home videos again,
the red, orange, and yellow
hang gliders launching

off the bluffs, the dust-green park,
grass spiked, electric.
I am at the center

untwisting myself.

I love the smell of napalm . . . : Remix

a golden shovel

Did I see napalm explode? All the time! Napalm
in the early days of the war. I was without a son—
—to that German convent! Nothing
was left of my grandfather's home. What else?
Where in my too-large hands? In
the hallway, Bê sang to him but couldn't calm the
word. Na Pom. Oh. Yes, the bombed world.
Here in Sài Gòn, her body still smells
of powdered milk. It was like
a spent match. When my wife woke from the coma, it was her smile that
swelled under my watch. Once, a South Vietnamese soldier, I
was diagnosed tim yêu. My body betrayed the love.
He was shot by the Việt Cộng. I watched. The
hospital had already buried—I remember my daughter's smell
of the damp paddy, I hear the voice of
thick, mucus-bright hair. Around her seemed a corona. Palm
reader predicted that I would suffer. In
my fists. Couldn't sleep last night. Who could sleep through a strafing, the
mud. I mapped our escape. We'd leave when the rain halted in the morning.

Heart of Darkness

a golden shovel

I learn endurance from my war-we-
ary father. We are watching war live
streamed: A girl grins despite the war in
Gaza, despite the war the-
n blasting another block. More war flicker-
ing on my cell phone. Between ads, war. May
slips into June, then July. Tents torched. War, it
quarrels over its own name. War last-
ing my lifetime and then more. War as-
h staticking the sky. August, September. The war long,
getting longer. It's genocide, not war, as
US-made bombs drop on every hospital. Genocide, not war. The-
ater of schools and refugee camps. For genocide, earth
retaliates. Hurricanes roar. Genocide keeps
on. Field executions. Genocide rolling
forward. October, November. We chant, Stop the genocide! But
the election presses on. Blue or red, it's genocide. Darkness
escalates, nearing winter. A poem, revolutionary, was.
echoing. A chorus for a revolution here.
Tomorrow, we'll sing how we won our revolution yesterday.

Dear child of the wind:

—past the sea and the green gullies, past the tangerine tree which you grew in the backyard, I knew you, in the taste of the flower stems you chewed, that tart summer scent of cut grass, I knew you in your bowl cut, the red car in the driveway, the lens of your father's eye.

Something recedes. Your father watched the stars materialize. Your mother left, your uncle was taken.

Your mother bought us a toilet seat on the ground. She bought concrete so that they could lift my bed above the floodwaters. She bought me medicine when I was dying, and when you came home, I knew you. I knew you, your American scents. I knew you, your pink tones. I knew you didn't know about my life, but you knew me by name.

Zombie Apocalypse Now: The Making of

Cue soundtrack.

The undead include
      my grandmother, my older sister,
      my uncle, who was a priest,
      four cousins, still children.

They eat the pomelos we set at the altar,
      all in a circle, peeling the membranes,
      dropping the segments
      into each other's mouths.

I am the director.

The zombies don't look like zombies.

Just my grandmother,
      unable to speak,
      the flies reanimating
      her body's giving up.

Just my older sister,
      a little Việt Cộng
      sacrificed to show
      the depravity of war.

I yell, *Cut!*—and they ascend into heaven.

Makeup! I shout across the set.

I ask the artists to bruise the undead.
I provide a mood board, sketches
composed by my brother,

happy to draw again. It's a family
production. My father fiddles
with the Super 8. He shakes his head

at the last reel: *Too dark.*
My mother in costume design,
head down at the sewing machine,

a measuring tape hanging from the curtain.
She is burning incense,
pouring holy water into the iron.

She stitches the tatters and hand-hems the silk.
She is careful, but we are running low on time.
The light is starting to dim.

I call down my uncle, my cousins,
their faces at the side of the road,
the red tableau.

I tell them,

> *Here is the script. Act natural.*
> *This is just like the story*
> *of your lives.*

Notes

In 1976, my parents were both cast as extras in Francis Ford Coppola's Vietnam War film *Apocalypse Now*.

I made collages, placing cutouts of my family's photos atop *Apocalypse Now* film stills in scenes where my parents specifically played extras on set.

The "Zombie Apocalypse Now" poems think about the overlap between zombie narratives and *Apocalypse Now*'s filming. In 2015, while watching the television series *The Walking Dead*, which is about a group of survivors trying to escape a zombie apocalypse, I began to speculate about what it would mean for my own family, the dead and the living, to tell this story ourselves.

The Walking Dead series ran from 2010 to 2022. One of the main characters, Glenn Rhee, was played by Steven Yeun. In watching the show, I was struck by the similarities between the experiences of the survivors in the show and my parents' experiences as refugees escaping the aftermath of a war.

In the poems marked *a golden shovel*, I use the golden shovel, a poetic form developed by Terrance Hayes, to take sentences from scripts written by Francis Ford Coppola and John Milius, using the words of these sentences as the last word of each line in a new poem.

"Bomb that tree line back about a hundred yards. Give me room to breathe" is dialogue spoken by Lieutenant Colonel Kilgore, played by Robert Duvall, in *Apocalypse Now*.

The poem "FADE IN: EXT." uses, for the final words in each line, the opening sentences of *Apocalypse Now Redux*, an original screenplay by John Milius and Francis Ford Coppola. Narration written by Michael Herr. Final Draft—A Transcription, first published in the United States 2001 by Talk Miramax books. First published in the United Kingdom in 2001 by Faber & Faber Limited. All rights reserved © 2001, Zoetrope Corporation.

FADE IN:

EXT. A SIMPLE IMAGE OF TREES - DAY

Coconut trees being VIEWED through the veil of time or a
dream. Occasionally colored smoke wafts through the FRAME,
yellow and then violet. MUSIC begins quietly, suggestive
of 1968–69. Perhaps "The End" by the Doors.

Now MOVING through the FRAME are skids of helicopters, not
that we could make them out as that though; rather, hard
shapes that glide by at random. Then a phantom helicopter
in FULL VIEW floats by the trees—suddenly without warning,
the jungle BURSTS into a bright red-orange glob of napalm
flame.

The VIEW MOVES ACROSS the burning trees as the smoke ghostly
helicopters come and go.

The poems titled "I love the smell of napalm . . ." use the following lines for their golden shovel end words: "Napalm, son. Nothing else in the world smells like that. I love the smell of napalm in the morning" (as spoken by Lieutenant Colonel Kilgore, played by Robert Duvall, in the theatrical release of *Apocalypse Now*).

The poem "December 3, 1975" uses for its golden shovel end words the *Apocalypse Now* draft from December 3, 1975 (original screenplay by John Milius, inspired by Joseph Conrad's novel *Heart of Darkness*; this draft by Francis Ford Coppola).

> It is very early in the dawn—blue light filters through
> the jungle and across a foul swamp. A mist clings to the
> trees. This could be the jungle of a million years ago.
>
> Our VIEW MOVES CLOSER, through the mist,
> TILTING DOWN to the tepid water.

Hearts of Darkness: A Filmmaker's Apocalypse is a 1991 American documentary film about the production of *Apocalypse Now*, begun by Francis Ford Coppola's wife, Eleanor Coppola.

"City of the Future" was an ekphrastic poem written after a postcard image printed by Kaya Press to celebrate the release of Sesshu Foster's book of the same name.

"Meals" adapts the following lines from Tiana Clark's *I Can't Talk About the Trees Without the Blood*: "I heard the wet click of little bones unfastening" (as "I hear the wet click of bones unfastening") and "Once, she dreamt she swallowed a snake" (as "Once I dreamt I was swallowed by a snake").

"Heart of Darkness" borrows its golden shovel end words from the following sentence from Joseph Conrad's *Heart of Darkness*: "We live in the flicker—may it last as long as the old earth keeps rolling! But darkness was here yesterday."

The following poems have been published, sometimes in different forms and versions and with different titles, in the following places:

"Becoming Ghost [I stand behind]": Poem-a-Day, Academy of American Poets

"Becoming Ghost [In Sài Gòn, I wore]": *The Offing*

"Zombie Apocalypse Now: The Walking Dead": Belladonna* chaplet

"*Bomb that tree line back about a hundred yards. Give me room to breathe.*": *Guernica*

"Becoming Ghost [Sundays, my parents drink]": *wildness*

"Cargo": *The Normal School*

"Go": *Poetry* magazine

"Zombie Apocalypse Now: Survival": *Blackbird*

"FADE IN: EXT.": *The Yale Review*

"In the kitchen, recounting": *Appocalips*, a three-channel video installation

"Becoming Ghost [I unhook the photograph]": *The Offing*

"December 3, 1975": *The Nation*

"Becoming Ghost [I lived]": *Coe Review*

"Q & A": *Litro Magazine*

"Dear America": 92nd Street Y's "A New Colossus" folio

"I love the smell of napalm . . . [From the hospital bed]":
   The New Republic

"The Extras' Commentary [I bought a tael of gold]": *Hyphen*

"Los Angeles, Manila, Đà Nẵng": Poem-a-Day, Academy of American
   Poets

"City of the Future": *Los Angeles Review of Books*

"Ode to": *wildness*

"Meals": *Los Angeles Review of Books Quarterly*

"Poem Before a Verdict": *Los Angeles Review of Books Quarterly*

"Zombie Apocalypse Now: Pandemic": *Hyphen*

"Zombie Apocalypse Now: Revival": *New England Review*

"Zombie Apocalypse Now: On Love": *New England Review*

"July is watermelon season.": Câylendar

"Zombie Apocalypse Now: Prelude": *Hyphen*

"Zombie Apocalypse Now: Documentary": *Poetry* magazine

"I love the smell of napalm . . . [Dow produced]": *The New Republic*

"Zombie Apocalypse Now: Talking Dead" (previously published as
   "I walked through the trees, mourning"): *Poetry* magazine

"Forgiveness": *New England Review*

"Dear child of the wind": *Litro Magazine*

"Zombie Apocalypse Now: The Making of": *Poetry* magazine

Acknowledgments

Thank you so much to my agents, Hafizah Geter and PJ Mark, at Janklow & Nesbit, who supported me throughout the book-making process. Thank you to my editor, Jenny Xu, and her team at Washington Square Press, including Ifeoma Anyoku, Maudee Genao, Sierra Swanson, Katie Rizzo, and Davina Mock-Maniscalco.

Thanks so much for the following organizations for providing space, time, community, and support for my work: Sundance Film Festival, Asian Cultural Council Grant, New York Foundations for the Arts Grant, New York State Council on the Arts Individual Artist Grant, Loghaven, The Shed, Ucross, Bread Loaf, Tin House, Monson Arts Residency, MacDowell, Sewanee Writers' Conference Fellow, Saltonstall Foundation for the Arts, Willapa Bay AiR, Djerassi, Kimmel Harding Nelson Center Residency, Anderson Center Residency, Montalvo Arts Center, Artist Trust Fellowship, Sierra Nevada College, Association for Asian American Studies, *The Asian American Literary Review*, Jerome Foundation, Lower Manhattan Cultural Council Workspace Residency, Kundiman, Cave Canem, Alice James Books, and Poets House.

Thanks to my friends, colleagues, mentors, and beloveds for providing myriad forms of writing support over the years: Kyle Lucia Wu, Sally Wen Mao, Christopher Radcliff, Laren McClung, Wo Chan, Monica Sok, Katie Bloom, Solmaz Sharif, Levi Rubeck, Paul Hlava Ceballos, Bianca Stone, R.A.

Villanueva, Helene Achanzar, Tiana Nobile, Jane Wong, Michelle Peñaloza, Eduardo Aguilar, April Naoko Heck, Christian Hawkey, Myung Mi Kim, The Grind, Matthew Olzmann, Mandy Marcus, Chrysanthemum, Seema Yasmin, Purvi Shah, Rana Tahir, Tariq Luthun, George Abraham, Jess Abughattas, Jennifer Chang, Oliver de la Paz, Lawrence-Minh Bùi Davis, Jess X. Snow, the Asian American Literature Festival Collective, Mahogany Browne, Ricardo Maldonado, Brian Truong, Jung Hae Chae, Hannah Bae, Cat Wei, Wilson Wong, Ocean Vuong, Kaveh Akbar, Diana Khoi Nguyen, Terrance Hayes, NYU's Creative Writing Program, Deborah Landau, Sharon Olds, Anne Carson, Yusef Komunyakaa, Matthew Rohrer, She Who Has No Master(s), Diasporic Vietnamese Artists Network, Viet Thanh Nguyen, Lan P. Duong, Alex Gallo-Brown, Jenne Lobsenz, SGV Food Club, Jean Chen Ho, Muriel Leung, Lisa Lee, Xochitl-Julisa Bermejo, Vickie Vértiz, Kenji C. Liu, Kien Lam, Soraya Membreno, Andrea Gutierrez, Ashaki Jackson, Neela Banerjee, Antioch MFA Program family, including Lisa Locascio Nighthawk, Alistair McCartney, Colette Freedman, Daisy Salas, Natalie Truhan, Colleen Bradley, and Max Delsohn, Murder of Crows Joseph Earl Thomas, Isle McElroy, Elias Rodriques, Nereida Trujillo, Gina Chung, Shirley Cai, Shan Rao, Rebecca John, Saifa Khan, Christie Louie, and Chaise Jones. Thank you to my neighbors Lorenzo Sanchez and Martha Sanchez for modeling love and generosity. If I have forgotten to name anyone, please forgive me.

Thanks, especially, to my family, who taught me everything I know about the pleasure, challenge, and necessity of storytelling: my mother Hoa Thi Le, my father Hue Nguyen Che, and my brothers, James Viet Che and Jean Long Che, and their partners, Linh Nguyen and Vivian Che. My grandmother, aunts, uncles, cousins, nieces, and nephews, my ancestors—the living and the dead.

About the Author

Cathy Linh Che is the author of *Split* (winner of the Kundiman Poetry Prize, the Norma Farber First Book Award from the Poetry Society of America, and the Best Poetry Book Award from the Association for Asian American Studies), *An Asian American A to Z: A Children's Guide to Our History*, and *Becoming Ghost*. Her video installation *Appocalips* is an Open Call commission with The Shed, and her film *We Were the Scenery* won the Short Film Jury Award: Nonfiction at the Sundance Film Festival.